THE BIG LIE

MEIN KAMPF REVISITED

By

DALE SPRINKLE

© 2004 by DALE SPRINKLE. All rights reserved.

No part of this book may be reproduced, stored in a retrieval system, or transmitted by any means, electronic, mechanical, photocopying, recording, or otherwise, without written permission from the author.

ISBN: 1-4140-5607-9 (e-book)
ISBN: 1-4140-5606-0 (Paperback)

This book is printed on acid free paper.

1stBooks - rev. 02/16/04

INTRODUCTION

A human-interest article appeared in a local newspaper concerning a high school student. In the article the student explained why she was proud to be a liberal Democrat. It was about her desire to see the government take a more active role in creating and enhancing fairness and equality in the country. She saw the Left as the philosophy interested in lifting the downtrodden and unfortunate poor, and the path toward eliminating prejudice. The inference was that the Right was at the root of many problems plaguing our society, representing the antithesis of freedom and fairness.

Why shouldn't a truly caring person feel this way? After all, the news has been replete with articles about the right wing Nazis and other right wing extremists causing problems in Germany, the U.S., and other countries. They attack people based solely on their race or religious affiliations. And hasn't it been "right wing dictatorships" or near dictatorships at the root of many of the century's problems? Recall Hitler? Mussolini's Fascists? Much of the outcry against the war in Vietnam was based on distaste for the "right wing" government of South Vietnam. Didn't a lot of people in the U.S. back the Sandinistas of Nicaragua as the lesser of evils, given the "right wing" extremes of the Contras? Juan Peron's dictatorship of Argentina was often labeled "right wing."

All of our lives in school, college, newspapers, magazines, and books we have heard or read that the term "dictatorship" is synonymous with "right wing." Regardless of how many people will embrace that term, "right wing dictatorship," it is THE big scam of the century. THE BIG LIE.

The Big Lie has been proffered to aid in the advance of the truly insidious political movement. The real dictatorial, oppressive, prejudice-promoting ideology. The ideology which manages to get good, proper thinking young high school people to embrace the philosophy which fostered the likes of Adolph Hitler, Joseph Stalin, and Mussolini.

No, you disagree? Then it's important that we explore facts. But first, the terms should be defined. That is, the right wing philosophy is that which is normally associated with political "conservatives," as generally found in the Republican Party. Its primary economic thrust is toward capitalism. The left is the philosophy referred to as liberal, as generally associated with the Democratic Party. This movement's thrust is away from capitalism and toward society or community ownership and operation of the means of production. These people believe that the government must play an active role in leveling the playing field and making things fair. That is, from each according to his ability, to each according to his need. The right wing sees the government in a much more limited role, mostly concerned with protection. The left, taken to its extreme, might properly be identified as socialism. The right, well, some say the extreme would be a dictatorship, such as we observed in Nazi Germany. Let's see:

The Nazi Party began as a part of the National Socialist German Workers' Party (NSDAP). In German: Nationalsozialistische Deutsche Arbeiterpartei, or Nazi for short.

Early in their existence, the Nazi leaders professed being socialists. In 1920, the German Workers' party held a now famous rally in a large Munich beer hall. There Hitler announced the party's programs, which included opposing capitalism, democracy, and especially the Jews.[1] Once in total control of Germany, the Nazi government instituted an economic policy of bureaucratic controls. Restraints were placed on imports, exports, prices, wages, and labor policies. Is it possible to imagine President Reagan pounding a podium and demanding more government control of business, or demanding that we replace capitalism with socialism? Socialism is LEFT wing. The Nazis were LEFT wing.

This book explores this subject in depth. Here we will deal with the real world. Facts will not be stumbling blocks that interfere with our theory. Many folks have The Big Lie and other misconceptions deeply embedded in their brains. These people are guided in their beliefs by slogans, not facts or good science. They have become "robotic sloganeers". Beware the robotic sloganeer! This book is an admonishment to those being influenced by the slogans to consider anew their validity. It is also a warning to the purveyors of garbage that the true and real world is still alive and its truth will prevail.

THE BOAT

Can you picture it? President Reagan rallying the people behind a loud and firm call for the government to cure the economy by taking over business and industry. How about Mr. Reagan drumming up support for his political career by urging his followers to join him in replacing capitalism with socialism? No indeed, Ronald Reagan is definitely not in that picture. Adolph Hitler was the leader who pushed those movements. So, how in the world have we come to describing both as "right wing?" Does a conservative Republican really have that much in common with a radical Socialist? What is the left, and what is the right?

A simple story clearly demonstrates the very basic philosophical foundations of the political left and right. Reference to this foundation will keep us on track as we explore The Big Lie.

The story involves two life rafts adrift in the ocean. There were five people on each raft. One had all left wingers aboard, the other all right wingers. Water rained from the heavens in sufficient quantities to negate any from dying of thirst. However, it was known (creative license) that starvation would prevail before rescue could occur. In the end, all the right wingers perished. Four left wingers survived to be rescued.

Those who survived did so by sacrificing one of their own. That is because they believed that the good of the majority outweighed the rights of an individual. Though under normal circumstances they would abhor killing, here the survival of the majority was superior to all perishing. That is, **the end justified the means.** All perished in the other boat because they believed in the **inalienable** right to life. That is, no collective (read government) can supercede this right, no matter how compelling the cause.

There is no intent here to indict those on the political left as cannibals. However, the illustration is accurate as to the very core of the two philosophies.

Liberalism is commonly considered a political movement that identifies with the left. Its name implies something new; some say a new movement into social justice. Many people who place themselves in this category, particularly students and recent grads, really feel that they are part of a new movement. A movement which is aimed at world harmony and peace.

Well, sorry folks, but the politics of the left has been around for most of the existence of civilization. Control of human activities and

THE BOAT

economics by a forceful entity (collectivist form of government) has been the norm. There have been some movements toward free enterprise and individual freedom. You know how you can identify those movements? How many new ideas, inventions, philosophers, and investigative journalists have come to the fore in socialist/dictatorial environments? What about democratic societies? Original thinking, scientific advances, and affluent societies are the by-products of political movements right, toward individual and market freedom. That is, a society where there are recognized INALIENABLE rights.

Not convinced? We have a vivid, real life modern example in our midst. This example has been very much in the news in the recent past, but not for its lesson in politics. Nonetheless, it is a lesson that should be like a mule, kicking us square in the head. Germany! Remember the cartoon in the papers after the "wall" went down? The one showing a West German driving a Mercedes Benz and an East German driving some dilapidated Eastern European car?

Think about it! Let's go back to 1946. There was Germany. People with a country, and not much else. To recover from its defeat in WWII, the whole nation truly had to start over from scratch.

The topography of Germany is generally: Mountains and foothills in the southern portion, agriculturally rich areas in the central area and toward the north, and manufacturing and seaports in the North. The political division of the Country

THE BIG LIE

following the war was north and south, creating East and West Germany. Obviously, both halves had about the same topography and natural resources. Both countries occupied an area about the size of California; thus the people were a rather homogeneous lot. That is, their education, customs, and life's experiences were very similar.

But look at what happened! Forty-five years later, the West is a shining star of prosperity and freedom. The East? When the dividing wall went down, the easterners journeyed into the West like children exploring a toy store for the first time. Numerous journalists and other observers who went there surmised that the East was 30 to 50 years behind the West.

Of course, some will observe that the West was helped out financially by the U.S. True, but of course the Soviet Union supported the East. Isn't it quite telling? Now West Germany is giving aid, not only to its eastern counterpart, but also to what was the Soviet Union. These socialist countries have fallen into economic ruin, much like that which befell post-war Germany. Only it hasn't been caused by losing a war, but rather by their collectivist economic policies. The economic policies of the left.

The ideals of the right may indeed result in all aboard a life raft perishing. But in the rest of life's experiences, it results in a free and prosperous society. Yes, the "liberal" idea that the best society is that which is guided by the will of the majority can have positive results. But when the "majority" is misguided or otherwise led by an evil

THE BOAT

government or person, the results can be terrible. History is replete with examples of societies doing terrible things in order to exercise the will of the majority. The nature of the left does allow for this to happen, because it does not recognize that there are absolute truths. So, **the end justifies the means.** Make no mistake! This is not a frivolous philosophical saying. It is the very heart of the left. The left wing does not function without the end justifying the means.

DICTATORS

The world has known more than a few dictators. But, are these born of the political right or left? What pictures come to mind when you hear the words: "right wing?" Don't you see booted troops goose-stepping down the boulevard? How about book burning parties, people being incarcerated for "wrong thinking," and minorities being pistol-whipped. Do we have enough collective fingers and toes to count the times you have read about "right wing dictatorships?" Probably not. Again, that IS the Big Lie.

What does it take to have a dictatorship? It requires a dictator, who has absolute power of government. There is no power in a government unless it can use its power to enforce its decrees. By its nature, it must be able to control its citizens absolutely. No citizen can have rights that are above the power of the dictator. A dictatorial government must be able to control all matters of the economy. There can be no "inalienable" right to property. The government must be able to suspend all private interests in property if it sees fit.

Hitler said it directly: "The movement advocates the principle of a Germanic democracy: the leader is elected, but then enjoys unconditional authority." And how would he bring the masses on board? "The nationalization of the broad masses can never be achieved by half-measures, but only by a ruthless and fanatically one-sided orientation toward the goal to be achieved." [2]

As to human rights: Many governments have called themselves "socialist" or "communist." Realistically it's very hard to distinguish them from outright dictatorships. But, it is, they say, the dictatorship of the proletariat. All of society owns equally the means of production. Practically, the operation of the means of production can not be accomplished by all of society simultaneously. The whole system will collapse unless someone or some group steps in to take control. Voila, a dictator is born. Witness: USSR, Cuba, China; socialist countries all.

OK, so modern-day liberalism does not want to go so far as to open the door for a dictator. They just want the government to take enough control to ensure that society and the means of production operate for the greater good of all folks equally. That is at the root of "liberalism." But how about when the "greater good" is determined to be the elimination of undesirable elements from

THE BIG LIE

the society? If the majority of the people, as represented by the heads of government, determine that Jews are the scourges of society, they can decide to eliminate them. While running for public office, Hitler's writings and speeches were replete with anti-Semitic rhetoric. He and his cohorts clearly stated that it was the Jews who were responsible for the pitiful condition of the German economy. He did get voted into power by a majority of the German people. Anti-Semitism was mandated. Remember: Five people in a life raft; one is sacrificed so that the majority may survive. It is ONLY this philosophy of the left that would allow for the Nazi holocaust. The philosophy of the right, with people having inalienable rights, would not allow for Hitler's ovens. And the economy: Can anyone imagine a dictatorship, socialism, or communism (whatever the differences are) not having total control of the means of production? If a dictator is to dictate, or the proletariat is to rule, there can be no individual inalienable right to property. In Socialism, the greater majority can only determine the "greater good". In a dictatorship, the dictator always has the last word.

So good, bad, or indifferent, dictatorships align with the "left." They do not allow for individuals to have private property rights superior to the rights of the government/dictator (that is, inalienable rights). Dictatorships are LEFT WING, though purposely misidentified as RIGHT WING. Some real life examples: The "right wing" Nazis, "right wing" dictators of Argentina, the "right wing"

DICTATORS

Somoza's of Nicaragua, and the "right wing" government of Diem (South Vietnam). These are glowing examples of The Big Lie. Let's dig deeper.

The Nazis of 1930's Germany identified themselves as socialists and espoused the principles of that ideology. In August 1934, following the death of President Paul von Hindenburg, 38 million Germans voted in favor of handing control of the German Government over to "the Fuhrer." Hitler thereby represented the majority of the people. He promised to create a new Germany by replacing democracy with the principles of leadership.[3] That the Nazis, as led by Hitler, were in complete control of the means of production is a fact beyond dispute. That they subsequently controlled the people via intimidation, incarceration, conscription, etc. is also common knowledge.

Did the Nazis believe that "the end justifies the means?" In Mein Kampf, Hitler, predicting how his movement could be successfully thrust into power, wrote that Nazism would unleash "a veritable barrage of lies and slanders against whatever adversary seems most dangerous, until the nerves of the attacked persons break down."[4]

After the people of Germany put the Nazis firmly in place, many policies and actions were adopted. From them we can examine if the majority recognized the inalienable rights of individuals (right wing), or if the will of the majority (elected Nazi Government) was seeking goals via any means (left wing).

THE BIG LIE

The goals of racial purity of the Reich were well publicized. The Ancestral Heritage Bureau became a part of the Nazi Government. It studied the racial origins of the German people. From it came the approved lists of mates for Nazis, particularly those belonging to the SS (the Party protection squad). Every SS man was "encouraged" to sire several children, whether in or out of wedlock. Approved young women became the League of German Girls, who were instructed in their duty to bear children for the Reich.[5] Marriage was not to be an obstacle. Homes were set up to house young girls who entertained SS men and bore their children. Note that the fathers of the children had no visiting privileges.

In the early 1930s, the German population included a small percentage of Jewish people. However, Nazi propaganda clearly blamed them for every problem that befell Germany following WWI. Jews were touted as being sub-human, yet somehow able to control much of what was happening in Germany. Minister of Popular Enlightenment and Propaganda, Joseph Goebbels stated, "The Jews are to blame for everything." One Nazi poster proclaimed "the Jew, purveyor of war, prolonger of war." A Berlin newspaper carried a story with a cartoon that depicted a Jew opening Pandora's Box, unleashing all the evils of the world.[6] How the Nazis handled this "problem of the Jews," is well known. The attempted genocide was a most blatant example of "the end justifies the means."

DICTATORS

Proof is in the language rules that were adopted for this operation: "The Final Solution," the official phrase for the project. "Evacuation for resettlement," meaning shipment of Jews to the death camps. "Special treatment," meaning the gassing. "Special installations," for the gas chambers. "Cleansing," for the killing. One visiting Nazi bureaucrat questioned the use of mass graves for the victims. SS Lt. General Globocnik informed him, "Gentlemen, if ever a generation should arise so slack and soft-boned that it cannot understand the importance of our work, then our entire National Socialism will have been in vain. I am of the opinion that bronze plaques should be erected with inscription to show that it was we who had the courage to carry out this great and necessary task." 7

So, the will of the majority in this Socialist regime was to create a master race by "selective breeding" and by exterminating a whole group of "undesirables." And this is labeled "right wing?" Clearly, it could only exist under the left-wing philosophies that the majority will is superior to inalienable rights to life, and that *the end justifies the means.*

Fascism in Italy had a beginning similar to that of Nazism in Germany. Its principal protracter was Benito Mussolini. As a young man he escaped military conscription by fleeing to Switzerland. He got involved with some young Marxists and even contributed some articles to Socialist newspapers. Returning to Italy, Mussolini led some anti-war demonstrations, desecrated the Italian flag, and

THE BIG LIE

was sent to prison. Upon his release, the Socialists hailed him as a new leader. He became the editor of a national Socialist daily paper. At the beginning of WWI, Mussolini first pushed for Italian neutrality, but later urged joining the Allied forces. His about face was secured by secret funds from other Allied countries. This money made it possible for him to found his own newspaper, which was referred to as "The Socialist Daily."

Great political maneuvering and constant about-facing in order to appeal to both sides of most issues marked the road to power in Italy for Mussolini and his Fascist Party. In the early days as Premier of Italy, Mussolini was very cautious. He stepped on as few toes as possible. He was well liked, and the country responded favorably. The incessant worker strikes subsided, and the economy grew. But Mussolini was not content to share the power of government with other elected factions. A new election law was pushed through, and the first election under it occurred in April, 1924. In a speech in a Government Chamber, a leader of the Socialists declared that the election was a fraud perpetrated by the Fascists. Mussolini denounced the speaker, who was found dead a few days later. Thereafter, the Fascists, led by Mussolini, assumed total control of the Italian Government. Civil liberties, including freedom of the press, ceased.

Adolf Hitler and Benito Mussolini were despots of the same stripe. Described by Mussolini as "the Rome-Berlin Axis," their abilities and methods of gaining and holding power had many similarities. They could enthrall large crowds with their assurances that they held the key to peace and prosperity. Their manipulation of cohorts was masterful. They could draw in people of power and position, use them, then crush them like so much trash. They both rose to power with the support of most of the people, who were beguiled by their great salesmanship. Each placed strong emphasis on their propaganda machines, while maintaining strong "police" forces to handle those not duped by the propaganda. Both hid their desires for power by projecting legitimacy and dignity. Both were born of Socialist ideals. Both ruled absolutely over civil and economic matters. Both exhibited strong beliefs in the end justifying the means. Both were manifestations of what the philosophy of the left wing can produce.

Clearly, the Argentina military dictatorship of Juan Peron was connected to the German Nazi Party. A November, 1998 article in Time International details the results of research by a truth commission established by Argentina President Carlos Menem. It told of the deep connections between Nazism and Ex-dictator Juan Peron. It is a history of political crimes, fascism, anti-Semitism, and concealment of ex-Nazis in Argentina since 1945.[8] Note that in 1960, Adolph Eichmann, the principal director of the "final solution" for the Third Reich, was captured in Argentina and removed to Israel.

In his book, "The Peron Era," Robert Alexander names and describes numerous Nazi

THE BIG LIE

and Italian fascist "escapees" who found refuge in Peron's Argentina. They included Otto Skorzeny, a close associate of Hitler and SS leader; Admiral Litzman, who commanded the German Black Sea Fleet; and Vittorio Mussolini, son of Il Duce.[9]

So what about this Argentina dictatorship? Up to 30,000 people were murdered during or just prior to the 1976-1983 "Dirty War" conducted by the military dictatorship.[10] A March, 1995 Newsweek article reported the confessions of former Argentina Naval Officer, Adolfo Francisco Scilinga, who admitted to executing 30 political prisoners by throwing them out of an airplane.[11]

As to economic factors: An economic study was done comparing the economic growth of 32 countries, several of them Latin American. The period covered was 1929 – 1983. Argentina was among those studied, and came in next to last, followed only by Honduras.

In 1947, President Peron pushed the Declaration of Economic Independence. Through that program, the Peron regime "clearly indicated that the regime has no qualms about government participation in economic affairs. Not only has it nationalized many of the country's basic industries, but it has also carried out a large program of government-directed economic development, and has set up several institutions for the purpose of exercising general supervision over the economy." [12]

Again, there was a government following the precepts of the German National Socialists (Nazis). Using any means to arrive at its goal of

DICTATORS

total control of the people and economy. The end justifying the means by which inalienable rights were subjugated to the power of the proletariat. Classic left wing.

The first Somoza (Tacho) was elected president of Nicaragua as the Nationalist Liberal party candidate in November, 1936. He gained that position by forcibly defeating the leading Sandinista, Sandino. Of course, the Sandinista have been labeled "left wing," and the press consistently referred to The Somoza regime as "right wing." Let's see:

Upon taking control of the government, Tacho Somoza and his family quickly became very rich. He instituted taxes and other schemes to bilk virtually every industry out of countless millions of dollars, as his reward for being president.[13] Somoza "concentrated his political skills on repressing the conservatives and strengthening his control over the Liberal Party. The powers of the Guard were also expanded, giving them control over internal revenue, communications, immigration, transportation, and even sanitation."[14] Tacho was assassinated in 1956. Other Somozas continued in power until they were ousted in 1979. It was the clergy, particularly Catholic priests, who alerted the world to the human rights violations and dictatorial practices of the government of Nicaragua.[15]

Oppression of human rights; control of the means of production (Somoza could not openly steal from an industrial complex that he didn't control), these can only exist in an environment

THE BIG LIE

which does not recognize the inalienable rights to life and property. These identify a political philosophy rooted in the LEFT. Again, can one see right wing President Reagan pressing to throw out the Constitution and taking control of industry? Hitler did, Peron did, Somoza did.

Some are confused by the fact that the Somozas were opposed by, and ultimately defeated by the Sandanistas, who were correctly labeled as "left wing." Surely then, the Somozas must be "right wing." No, that one "left wing" regime would be ousted by another "left wing" regime is neither uncommon nor surprising.

Who can forget the vehement opposition to this country's involvement in the Vietnam War? Some of that was purely a matter of being against war, per se. But so much of the opposition was out of disgust for backing the oppressive "right wing" government of Diem, et.al. Backing the Diem regime was indeed hard to justify, but was Diem "right wing?"

Diem visited the US for several years prior to his rise to power in South Vietnam. During that time, he courted, or should I say he associated with a number of political leaders. No doubt he was interested in selling his "cause," so that the US would back his power play. It is interesting to note that he usually associated with liberal Democrats. Though, of course, it was the Republican government of President Eisenhower that ultimately did lend its support to Diem.

Prior to the US involvement there, Vietnam had been rocked by war, virtually for generations.

DICTATORS

Much of the problem was the objection to French colonialism, though there were other groups with agendas helping stir the pot. One of those groups was the Vietnamese Communist Party. They did not advocate a strong Marxist regime. Rather, they appealed to the Vietnamese peoples' long-standing feelings against colonialism, and their desire for independence. Ho Chi Minh proclaimed: "We hold the truths that all men are created equal, that they are endowed by their creator with certain inalienable rights, among which are life, liberty, and the pursuit of happiness."[16] Of course, the atrocities committed against their own people are an undeniable legacy of those Communists. But at the time, that Party did indeed appeal to the masses, and collected a significant following. But, there was also a significant number of Vietnamese who were strongly anti-Communist. These warring factions did, however, all share a strong feeling of anti-colonialism. A respite from their war was realized in the 1950s, via a Geneva agreement that divided the country into North and South Vietnam. That agreement also provided for a unification election aimed at bridging this rift.

In the late 1940s and 50s, the US was bent on stopping the spread of Communism, particularly in Southeast Asia. Communism was gaining ground in Vietnam, so that seemed like the perfect place to oppose it. Diem was a sycophant to US politicians and professed to have followings in his anti-Communist and anti-French agendas. He was viewed as the best banner-carrier for the

THE BIG LIE

US anti-Communist effort, since his feelings toward the French would give him wide appeal.

Wide appeal indeed. In an October 1955 election, Diem came to power in Vietnam by winning 98.2 percent of the vote. But did Diem oppose Communism because he felt that it would be in his country's best interest to have a right wing government? A government which recognizes its citizens' inalienable rights to life, liberty, and property? Or did he use his anti-Communism to elicit US support so that he could substitute his dictatorial power for that of the Communists, with the idea of dominating the country?

Once in office, Diem moved quickly to set up his power machine to solidify his control of Vietnam. The unification election, specified in the Geneva accord, never occurred. In the urban areas, Diem rounded up political opponents of every stripe. Political prisoners numbered in the tens of thousands, with an estimated 12,000 killed during the period 1955-57.[17] One opposition group issued a manifesto indicting the Diem regime claiming that, "Continuous arrests fill the jails and prisons to the rafters...public opinion and the press are reduced to silence." Many of the people behind this decree where imprisoned. All domains of society felt the oppressive hand of the Diem government.

Rural areas were harder to control. Diem would first round up those people identified as being members of village councils. Next he intimidated religious leaders to support him.

DICTATORS

Those that couldn't be convinced were arrested and taken away. Diem set up a network of province chiefs. They were authorized to "execute suspects without a hearing or even a police record."[18] He tried to keep the people off-balance with population transfers.

This political and religious repression was done under the banner of "anti-Communism." By that, Diem continued to receive US support. This was another example of *the end justifies the means*; a left-wing banner carried to justify negating individuals' inalienable rights to life and property.

As to economic issues: The economic policies of Diem showed him to be anti-capitalist and anxious to gain personal wealth. National industries covered most sectors of the means of production. Private investment in those means of production was negated. This caused consternation among some US leaders, but Diem continued to receive support due to his anti-Communist stance (that is, Diem sought to eliminate the Communist Party. There is a difference). Diem learned how to control the trade market, as well as artificially influence monetary exchange rates. Suffice it to say that Diem did not employ Ronald Reagan style laissez faire economics. His economic policies were clearly far to the left, employing government control of nearly every aspect of the economy.

From Nazi Germany, through South American dictatorships, to Vietnam, weaves a common thread that identifies these regimes as *right wing*.

THE BIG LIE

That is that they each opposed some political movement that was readily identified as *left wing*. They each professed to oppose Communism. So did that opposition then qualify them to be labeled *right wing?* No, all that oppose Communism are not right wing. The regimes we have looked at were really interested in **replacing** Communism. That is, the Communists wielded a certain amount of power/control over certain areas. The dictatorships did not really oppose Communism on a philosophical basis. They simply wanted to replace the dictatorship of the Communists with their own dictatorship. If two liberal Democrats run for President against each other in the primaries, does it follow that one is liberal and the other conservative? No, one just wants the other's voter support.

And speaking of Communism. By most accounts, the 1960s Cultural Revolution in China was labeled a radical "left wing" movement. Studying the history of Mao Zedong's rise to power and that subsequent "Revolution", one can not help but see the similarities with Hitler's rise to power and the brutal deployment of the Nazi movement (an excellent read on this is Li Zhensheng's "Red Color News Soldier: A Chinese Photographer's Odyssey Through The Cultural Revolution."). Yet, one is right and the other left?

Is everyone who considers his or her political philosophy as left, or liberal, really a latent Nazis? No, I am certain that most such people are horrified when they hear details of the atrocities committed by that regime. But this inspires

DICTATORS

recollection of a lady I met some years ago. She was in her seventies when we became acquainted. I soon learned that she was a very kind person, with a heart of gold. She truly had no prejudices; she accepted all manner of folks on their own merit.

How surprised I was to learn about her background. She was born and raised in Germany, and while a young lady, she served in the Army. The Nazi Army. After I got to know her well enough to ask, I inquired as to what she thought about the atrocities visited upon the Jews. I pointed out that she has talked very fondly about some acquaintances who are Jewish. She denied ever harboring any anti-Semitism. She explained, much to my satisfaction, that neither she nor her late husband (who was also in that Army), nor anyone she knew were aware of the death camps. She pointed out that the German press supported Hitler, and therefore printed only what was politically correct.

The real point here is not whether or not she knew what was going on in the death camps. The point is that Hitler came to power ONLY with the support of the people. He espoused liberal platforms that were promises that he and the Government were going to make things better for each individual. They had only to turn control over to the Party, and things would get better. That is left wing politics. This lady, and many many others like her, supported these liberal platforms. They supported left wing politics that as we have seen above is used to justify all sorts of dictatorial

THE BIG LIE

policies, including death to political opponents and "undesirables."

The philosophy of the right, that there are inalienable rights that cannot justifiably be denied by any means, does not allow for these dictatorial regimes. Again, a dictator cannot exist without having power over the means of production AND over the rights of individuals. If people are left wing, and do not want these atrocious dictatorships to arise, they have to change their politics. You may be kind and devoid of prejudice and malice toward any person, but if you support the tenants of left wing politics you acquiesce to any horrible political acts which may feed on your philosophy.

WHY THE LIE?

"The basic tenets of my political philosophy are the same as the Nazis'; how cool!" No indeed, we won't expect to hear that sentence uttered very often. Would that explain why the press, textbooks, college profs, politicians, et.al. continually mislabel the historically horrible dictatorial political movements, and their followers, as *right wing*? Are they using "right wing" to describe a particular political philosophy or philosophies, or are they simply using "right wing" to describe any movement gone awry?

The canons of Socialism and Communism provide that the good of the majority, as the majority perceives that good, outweighs any inalienable rights an individual may claim. That the end justifies the means is an integral part of those political philosophies. The lessons of history clearly show that the dictatorship of the proletariat and any other nature of dictatorship share a legacy of oppression of people through violence,

THE BIG LIE

incarceration, and confiscation of private property, all under the guise of *the end justifying the means*. So is that right wing or left wing?

Anyone proud of being a compassionate liberal would want to distance his or her political beliefs as far from the Nazis as possible. But when the fact is that your political foundation is identical with and is the exact justification for the success of these dictatorships, you have a problem. What to do?

As long as you are left wing and therefore your political philosophy allows that the end justifies the means, there is no problem. The "desirable" end of showing that the troubles of this world originate from your opposition's politics allows you to lie. Hitler consistently and constantly blamed the woes of post-war Germany on the Jews. He knew that that was not true. He knew that it was losing WWI and subsequent bureaucratic corruption and bungling which were to blame. He knew that those events came about because of the expansionist desires of a prior powerful German government. But he truly believed that he could orchestrate a recovery and subsequent ascension to greatness of the Fatherland and the "Aryan Race." He viewed that end as good, so whatever means he had to use to achieve it were justified. Blaming the Jews provided a rallying point for his ascension to power. Hitler was a Socialist – a left wing politician.

Is there a BIG LIE in this Country? Has the "right wing" label been falsely applied to "left wing" movements and philosophies? Though one might

WHY THE LIE?

answer, "DUH," in keeping with the latest language idioms, proof will be presented:

Some might recognize the name Jackson Spielvogel from a college history class. He is a historian of some note, with an impressive list of credentials. He is the author of some history texts, including volumes of "Western Civilization," which are required reading in some college history classes.

In "Western Civilization, volume II, Second Edition," the author wrote about the rise of "modern totalitarian" states following WWI: "Dictatorship was by no means a new phenomenon, but the modern totalitarian state was. The totalitarian regimes, whose best examples can be found in Stalinist Russia and Nazi Germany, extended the functions and power of the central state far beyond what they had been in the past...The modern totalitarian state might have begun as an old-fashioned political dictatorship, but it soon moved beyond the ideal of passive obedience expected in a traditional dictatorship or authoritarian monarchy. The new "total states" expected the active loyalty and commitment of citizens to the regime's goals. They used modern mass propaganda techniques and high-speed modern communications to conquer the minds and hearts of their subjects. The total state aimed to control not only the economic, political, and social aspects of life, but the intellectual and cultural as well...The modern totalitarian state was to be led by a single leader and a single party. It ruthlessly rejected the liberal

THE BIG LIE

ideal of limited government power and constitutional guarantees of individual freedoms. Indeed, individual freedom was to be subordinated to the collective will of the masses, organized and determined for them by a leader or leaders."[19]

It would do well here to ponder this historical analysis. Are we talking "right wing" i.e., inalienable rights to life, liberty, and property? A free enterprise system such as that sought by Reagan conservatives? The life raft where all perish? Or does this mostly fit in the "left wing" mode; dictatorship of the proletariat; the end justifies the means; the life raft with four survivors?

Reading on in this text, the author states: "Fascism in Italy and Nazism in Germany grew out of extreme rightist preoccupations with nationalism and, in the case of Germany, with racism. Communism in Soviet Russia emerged out of Marxian socialism, a radical leftist program. Thus, totalitarianism could and did exist in what were perceived as extreme right wing and left-wing regimes. This fact helped bring about a new concept of the political spectrum in which the extremes were no longer seen as opposites on a linear scale, but came to be viewed as being similar to each other in at least some respects."[20]

Hogwash! Nationalism does not point right or left. A country can be nationalistic and still be very democratic and respectful of the rights of individuals. Nationalism can also exist in a country that is dictatorial and totally without

WHY THE LIE?

individual rights. The German and Italian totalitarianism came from the same basic political spectrum as did the Stalinist dictatorship. That is the LEFT WING. First and foremost there has to be the total acceptance that the end justifies the means. There has to be no recognition that there are inalienable rights to life, liberty, or property. Whether they were nationalistic, homophobic, black or white, Jew or Gentile, or red headed was immaterial. These totalitarian regimes came to power rooted in and propelled by the philosophies of the left. Had they been right wing, they could not have risen to power over the backs of peoples' inalienable rights.

But, of course, college students have here been informed that Nazism and Italian Fascism were "right wing" movements. Are there readings they will encounter that will correct this fallacy? Well, no. Members of today's Press, being primarily "left wing" themselves (see subsequent chapters), certainly do not want to correct the illusion that the nasty regimes of the past were "right wing." Here are some examples:

In the September 25, 2000 <u>US News and World Report</u>, David E. Kaplan, Lucian Kim, and Douglas Pasternak authored an article entitled, "Nazism's New Global Threat." The article is an excellent overview of the current Nazi movement, including their ties to the KKK, Hammerskin Nation, National Alliance, and Angry Aryans. It starts with the story of Hendrik Mobus, a neo-Nazi who had been convicted of murder in Germany. After violating parole he fled to the US, where he

THE BIG LIE

helped "gatherings of the **far right.**" It continues by stating that German officials say some 54,000 individuals are tied to "the **extreme right** in that country," with 100,000 to 200,000 Americans believed to have similar ties.

The article tags the Hammerskin Nation as being among the most active new-Nazi groups. They are described as a "federation of so-called skinheads whose members sport swastikas along with their shaved heads and steel-toes boots." They are known for their violence, and have worldwide chapters. "If the American **radical right** has an unofficial ambassador, though, it is William Pierce," leader of the National Alliance. Pierce wrote the novel, "Turner Diaries." That novel "depicted an American race war in which the US Government is overthrown and Jews and minorities are systematically slain." (The end justifies the means – no inalienable rights to life. What political philosophy are we looking at here?). The article continues by describing Pierce as sounding "like Adolph Hitler in 1933." (Remember Hitler in 1933: proclaiming to follow the ideals of National Socialism and blasting capitalism). The article concludes with a description of the Angry Aryan and the National Alliance as neo-Nazi groups **"on the far right."**

There are more examples of the Press promoting the Big Lie: The New Republic, May 29, 1995, carried an article by Richard Stengel titled, "White Right: The South African Nexus." The article is a description of a paramilitary South African group, they term "white right," known as

WHY THE LIE?

AWB (Afrikaner Resistance Movement), et.al. The movement is described as being similar to "American militia movements." They are engaged in bombings. They are linked to the National Front, in England, and National Socialists in Germany. Particularly the AWB, they are well organized and well armed. They are known to have committed a number of robberies. They share "the American **far-right's** paranoia about Jewish bankers..."

So these National Socialists (aka neo-Nazis) share a paranoia with the American **right** about Jewish bankers? Truth is, there are "right wing" Jewish people in the Republican Party who are in the banking industry. Mr. Stengel, you are misleading people.

Still more: From Knight-Ridder/Tribune News Service, June 12, 1998: "Right wing movement's success in Germany called "tip of the iceberg," by Lori Montgomery: This article describes a serious nationalistic movement in Germany. "**Right wing** hate crimes are rising, particularly attacks on foreigners, left-wingers, the homeless, and handicapped." It describes the rise of the **right-wing** German People's Union (DVU) as "neo-Nazi."

Recognizing peoples' inalienable right to life, liberty, and property does not allow for "hate crimes." Believing your cause just, and accepting that the end justifies the means, does allow for hate crimes. Though hate crimes are a bit twisted for most people on the ideological left, they are nevertheless born of the left.

THE BIG LIE

The Wall Street Journal does not escape. In the August 25, 2000 edition, in the "What's News – World Wide" column: Two German banks plan on closing accounts held by "the **far-right** National Democratic Party." That has caused debate as to how to crack down on "racist violence."

New York Times, September 15, 2000, Page A6, by Victor Homola (NYT): This article told of Germany banning "the **far-right** group Blood and Honor for spreading neo-Nazi propaganda..." It further reported that the group "has ties to the larger **far-right** German National Democratic Party.

From a local paper in November, 2000, an Associated Press by-line reads, "Berlin **rightist** march spurs clash." The article described a demonstration by 1,400 "**extreme rightists**" who were demonstrating in protest of plans to outlaw "the **far-right** National Democratic Party." There were "three **far-right** activists" arrested. Opposition protestors carried signs stating "No to neo-Nazis", etc. "The **far-right** protesters had originally planned to march through the Brandenburg Gate, once used by Nazi parades. About 3,600 police were on duty in anticipation of clashes at the second **far-right** march in Berlin this month."

This article contained 8 paragraphs. It would be safe to say that the author(s) went overboard to describe these "neo-Nazis" as "right wing." That is called "propaganda!" Repeating a lie over and

WHY THE LIE?

over to ensure that it will convince those who don't know better.

Another <u>Associated Press</u> article in the same paper, a few days later: "**Far-right** teens arrested in vandalism." This piece told of two teen-agers being arrested for vandalizing a memorial, which was one of several "weekend incidents in east Germany involving **extreme rightists.** The kids were caught trying to affix a sticker of the **far-right** National Democratic Party." Next paragraph: "Both boys had known **far-right** ties…". Two more paragraphs: "…about 60 miles farther south, some 180 **far-right** skinheads…threw bottles at police arriving to break up" an event..

The point is clear. Educators and the Press have been and are continuing to tell The Big Lie. The fact is, most of us have heard the Nazis and other dictatorships referred to as "right wing" or "far right" for so long and so often that it is tough to think otherwise. Even with a rational and factual exposure of the Lie, it is hard to say, "left wing Nazi," "neo-Nazis on the left," "far-left radical skinheads," etc. It is hard because of the old axiom: If you repeat a lie often enough, it will become accepted as truth.

PRESS

It is not possible to say too much about the complicity of the Press in promoting The Big Lie. Much has been declared, and denied, about the left wing prejudices of the Press. If folks with left wing political leanings heavily populate the Press, it would become clear why they would want to promote The Big Lie at every turn. Again, that is if your basic political philosophy dovetails with that of the Nazis, et.al., you would want to do all you can to dispel that truth. You might lie to your readers, your friends, your mother, and most of all, to yourself. Only after you have told or repeated *the lie* often enough to make it appear to be the truth, even to yourself, can you feel good about the basis for your political philosophy.

Much as we all, left and right, despise Hitler and his Nazi movement, we all must admit that Hitler possessed a sort of genius for doing what he did. What he did was gain the confidence of masses of people, while blatantly using their

PRESS

confidence to gain control over them. Ultimately he controlled one of the largest, deadliest single military machines the world has ever known. A careful perusal of the events of World War II clearly show that but for some major military blunders by Hitler and his high command, we could all be chanting "sieg heil" today. Hitler may have blundered militarily, but his ability to gain control of people was masterful, and continues to work today as his movement lives on.

So what does this have to do with the Press? Well, let's listen to Hitler on the subject. From Mein Kampf: "By far the greatest share in their political education, which in this case is most aptly designated by the word "propaganda," falls the account of the press. It is foremost in performing this "work of enlightenment" and thus represents a sort of school for grownups… At first I could not help but be amazed at how short a time it took this great evil power within the state to create a certain opinion even where it meant totally falsifying profound desires and views which surely existed among the public. In a few days a ridiculous episode had become a significant state action, while, conversely, at the same time, vital problems fell a prey to public oblivion, or rather were simply filched from the memory and consciousness of the masses… He will poke into the most secret family affairs and not rest until his truffle-searching instinct digs up some miserable incident which is calculated to finish off the unfortunate victim. But if, after the most careful sniffing, absolutely nothing is found, either in the

THE BIG LIE

man's public or private life, one of these scoundrels simply seizes on slander, in the firm conviction that despite a thousand refutations something always sticks and moreover, through the immediate and hundredfold repetition of his defamations by all his accomplices, any resistance on the part of the victim is in most cases utterly impossible; and it must be borne in mind that this rabble never acts out of motives which might seem credible or even understandable to the rest of humanity."[21] Anything sound familiar here?

Hitler commented on his intended use of the Press: "Propaganda in the War was a means to an end, and the end was the struggle for the existence of the German people…for even propaganda is no more than a weapon, though a frightful one in the hand of the expert."[22] "It is a means and must therefore be judged with regard to its end. It must consequently take a form calculated to support the aim which it serves…"[23]

Powerful stuff! What about our present day Press? If it is serving to objectively report the news, it is fulfilling its purpose. If it is acting in the manner Hitler spoke of, that is, serving a political agenda, then it is not fulfilling its purpose. Rather, it is then a tool of propaganda with a political agenda. If the Press is such a tool, a "frightful one" at that, it is evil. That is, if the members of the Press are using it to further their own political agenda, they are propagandizing the public. They are working toward an end, using an evil means. It is evil because by its very nature, propaganda

PRESS

is evil. If it were the truth, or based on truth, it would not be propaganda. If news stories are carried straight up, the truth will prevail in the minds of the readers, and truth and facts will motivate their political convictions. If news stories are manipulated to favor a political ideology, then they are meant to "totally falsify profound desires and views that surely existed among the public." When political agendas have to be promoted by propaganda, not the facts, oppression is sure to be the byproduct. If not, then what purpose does propaganda serve? Truth and reality will always lead the way to freedom. Lies and manipulations of the truth only need to exist to further an evil cause which people would not tolerate if they knew the truth.

Basically, if a vendor has a good product to sell, he or she will surely tell the truth about it. If the vendor is trying to sell you a real piece of junk, then surely you will be fed lies about the product, or at least the truth will be manipulated to misrepresent it. Again, propaganda is only necessary to sell evil.

There have been some objective studies of the Press in this country which have revealed much as to their political makeup. In the 1980s, the Los Angeles Times polled 3,000 newspaper reporters and editors. Fifty-five percent described themselves as liberal, and 17% as conservative. Only 26% of the journalists voted for Reagan in 1984, when he got 59% of the electorates' votes. "William C. Adams, a professor of public administration at George Washington University,

THE BIG LIE

found that television reports on the 1984 Democratic and Republican conventions came by a 7-1 margin from the liberal agenda."[24]

Robert and Linda Lichter and Stanley Rothman conducted a very in-depth objective study of the politics of the Press. The study looked at political attitudes of journalists at America's leading national media. That is: New York Times, Washington Post, Wall Street Journal, Time, Newsweek, US News and World Report, television networks ABC, CBS, and NBC, and public television. The results found these institutions replete with journalists who were overwhelmingly liberal.

In their study, the Lichters and Rothman found that newspapermen educated in the school of hard knocks were a dying breed. Taking their place are journalists who are being educated in the elite universities.[25] From a Reader's Digest article: "We no longer represent a wide diversity of views," columnist Joseph Kraft wrote in 1981, "Instead, today's journalists bring to their jobs a homogeneous political and social outlook – liberal, anti-establishment and secular."[26]

The Lichter/Rothman study included some telling numbers. Regarding voting records of journalists: From 1964 through 1976, their support of the Democratic candidate never fell below 80%. In 1972, 60% of the public voted for Nixon, while 80% of the media elite voted for McGovern. The same margin was present in the Carter – Ford election. In 1964, journalists picked Johnson over Goldwater, 94 to 6 percent. Across four elections, elite journalists' selection of the Democratic candidate was 30 to 50 percent greater than among the entire electorate.

The same study looked to the future of journalism. They conducted surveys at the prestigious Columbia University's Graduate School of Journalism. That student survey showed 85% claimed to be liberal, and 11% conservative. "These elite journalism school students are at least as critical of traditional social and cultural mores as today's leading journalists...The students' strongest disapproval is reserved for conservative groups and individuals. Seventy-eight percent disapproved of Ronald Reagan...They rated Cuban Premier Fidel Castro...considerably more positively than Ronald Reagan."[27]

Summarizing, the study's authors observed that today's leading journalists are politically liberal. Those characteristics will likely become more pronounced in the future. Moreover, students at the prestigious Columbia School of Journalism take a quantum leap beyond their elders in criticizing America's economic and political institutions. They also profess admiration for liberal public figures and media organizations, but disapprove of conservative newsmakers and news outlets.

Does news journalism draw in people from the political left, or do people from the left move toward such journalism in order to further their political agenda? It would seem that reporting the news as a career would not have a political

THE BIG LIE

motivation. Why should it draw from one political ideology more than from another? That is unless it is true that activists on the left purposefully choose to enter the Press in order to further their agenda, rather than objectively report the news. Hmmm!

So what? I hear someone say. As long as they honestly and impartially report the news, what difference does it make what an individual journalist's political philosophy is? At this point, having been an avid observer of the Press for decades, I break into uncontrolled laughter. Oh, there are some journalists who deny the liberal bias of the Press. So, instead of simply accepting the glaring fact of that bias, the subject should be explored further.

We turn to The Mini Page, a weekly supplement distributed by Universal Press Syndicate. This supplement is included in some daily newspapers. It is in color, with large type, and illustrated with children and cartoon characters. It is obviously intended for children. It explores a variety of subjects including science, the environment, and hints for living and learning. In the September 4, 2001 edition, instruction was given on how to read and learn. A major part of the edition was titled, "How to Be a Newspaper Reader." The thrust of that article was learning how to "Zip-Zip-Zip," or skimming the "headlines for a short summary of each story." The author noted that, "News stories are written to make skimming easier."

PRESS

So, let's try this skimming method of reading the paper. August 28, 2001, the Bangor (Maine) Daily News...the front page – major headline: "Social Security tap likely". The sub: "Budget update predicts $9 billion withdrawal." (by Curt Anderson, The Associated Press). The first paragraph: "WASHINGTON – The sour economy and President Bush's tax cut will force the government to tap $9 billion in Social Security reserves this year, congressional analysts concluded in a report Monday, igniting a bitter political fight over the dwindling surplus."

OK, we've skimmed the story. Obviously, President Bush's tax cut is going to cost the Social Security system billions of dollars, right? Same newspaper; Letters to the Editor, September 4, 2001: Letter titled, "Hard-earned money." A Bangor lady laments, "Recently, it was reported that President Bush is planning (saying that it has to be done) to use the Social Security surplus to help the government pay its obligations...What does the government of this country think retired folks are going to have to look forward to after their hard-earned money goes for no one knows what? President Bush, have a nice day."

Apparently this reader skimmed the August 28 story. Did that skimming properly inform her? Her letter certainly reflects the headlines and lead paragraph. So what else would one learn by not skimming that article? Well, first off, the whole article involves projections. The idea of taking $9 billion from Social Security surpluses is actually

THE BIG LIE

reported as a "pessimistic projection from the nonpartisan CBO." That did not come from the President. Following the story onto subsequent pages we learn: "House Minority Leader Dick Gephardt, D-Mo. said the 10 year $1.35 trillion tax cut is causing an alarming fiscal crisis, draining away the surplus cushion just as the economic downturn is hitting home. The CBO provides the budget numbers Congress is required to use. The numbers don't lie, Gephardt said. OK, so the budget crisis continues, and one might well get the impression that Social Security is in real trouble. Is that really true? Let's move further into the article. "The CBO now projects the total budget surplus for the fiscal year that ends Sept. 30 at $153 billion. That is down $122 billion from its May estimate but still an enormous amount." Toward the end of the story, "Over the next 10 years, the CBO is forecasting a $3.4 trillion surplus counting Social Security, down from $5.6 trillion in its May forecast. The tax cut and the associated changes in interest costs account for more than $1.7 trillion of the surplus reduction." (Note, this **projection** can not take into account that most people will not place their tax cut money into a coffee can and bury it. If in fact they spend or invest it, surely the outcome will not be as per the projections). Fact is, this year's Social Security surplus is the second largest in history, at about $157 Billion. Look back now to the headlines and first paragraph. Do they really reflect the gist of the story, which truly involved some **early** speculation about possible reductions

PRESS

in tremendous **overages?** Note what the letter writer thought!

Remember the sharp rise in gasoline prices in the spring of 2001? Prices particularly escalated in California, where rumors abounded of approaching $3 per gallon. The McClatchy Newspapers did not miss the opportunity to propagandize. Once again, **skimming** the paper for May 8, 2001, the following jumps out: "(headline) **Bush won't cut gas taxes**. (Subhead) President has no plan to intervene as prices soar at the pump. By James Rosen, Bee Washington Bureau. (first paragraph) **WASHINGTON** – President Bush has no plans to lower the federal gasoline tax or take other steps to help motorists despite fuel prices that hit a record national average price Monday and likely will surge higher during the peak summer travel season."

Anyone recall the furor raised in subsequent months toward President Bush's plans to open more oil drilling fields? Hands please. Actually, if one reads further into this story, they will find a statement from the White House press secretary explaining that Bush is focusing on "long term solutions, not quick fixes." Reading on, we find it mentioned that the Federal gas tax is 18 cents per gallon. Doing a little math: 18-cent tax is but 10% of the common pump price of about $1.80 per gallon. So if the tax were cut by a whopping 50%, we could all rejoice with a 5% reduction in price? It's interesting to note that much of the Press has frequently attacked the President for

THE BIG LIE

his tax reduction measures. Here he is castigated for **not** reducing taxes, which reduction would have had a negligible impact (on the pump price of gasoline).

The real significance with this story is the message given to those of us who skim the newspaper. "President has no plan to intervene<u>…or take other steps</u> to help motorists…" That, of course, was a blatant lie. As explained deeper into the article, he did have plans; they just didn't involve the quick fix suggested, which truly would have been no fix at all. Printed at the beginning of the story **the lie** was aimed to catch the bulk of us, as we skim the paper for news. Hitler would have been proud!

The coverage of the recently completed presidential election (2000) affords some more looks at the bias of the Press. Actually, it seemed that the Press was more prone to attack the Republican vice-presidential candidate (Richard Cheney) than the presidential candidate. In fact, Cheney's public life became well known, via all the Press coverage given him. On the other hand, when the campaigning was completed, I realized that I knew practically nothing about Joseph Lieberman, the Democratic vice-presidential candidate.

A headline in a McClatchy newspaper in August, 2000 read: "Fed contracts boosted Cheney-led company." The subhead was, "Bush has blasted that type of military spending." The story was by Karen Gullo, Associated Press. Obviously, the point of the story was to depict a

PRESS

rift in political interests between Mr. Bush and his running mate. The text pointed out that a company formerly headed by Mr. Cheney received $2 billion in federal contracts to provide supplies for troops on some peace keeping missions. That is, "U.S. deployments in Bosnia, Kosovo, Somalia and elsewhere – the kinds of missions Bush has pledged to reduce if elected…" Now, Mr. Bush has pledged to be more reluctant to send US troops on peacekeeping missions, which of course indicated a criticism of President Clinton's propensity to send troops on such missions. This IS NOT a criticism of the companies that outfitted the troops. I feel very positive that Mr. Bush has never blamed a corporation that provided supplies for troops with ordering military actions. Mr. Bush blasted those types of military ACTIONS, not the act of supplying the missions. **The story was, in fact, a lie.** The end justifies the means?

The same newspaper, September 9, 2000. The headline: "Cheney's failure to vote, company restroom policy questioned." The story was by Megan Garvey and Mark Z. Barabak, Los Angeles Times. Though Mr. Cheney stated that he has voted in every general election over the past 22 years, he was criticized for not voting in many local Texas elections. This would be a more meaningful question if the home-state voting records of other candidates were detailed. I wonder if the Vice President and Senator Lieberman voted in all hometown elections while serving in Washington?

THE BIG LIE

    The article went beyond the headlines to state, "Moreover, the latest revelations increased griping among Republicans about the series of side issues Cheney has visited upon the Bush campaign..." Who are those Republicans, when did they make such statements? Is this a NEWS statement or an EDITORIAL statement? Or is it just a lie? So what are some of the revelations referred to here? One was "Cheney has been forced to explain...a vote against a resolution calling for the release of Nelson Mandela from a South African prison." In the past Mr. Cheney had been asked about that vote. He explained that that 1986 measure included a resolution to recognize the African National Congress. The ANC was then identified as a terrorist organization. So, a yes vote had no legal weight to free Mr. Mandela, but it would have caused this country to give legitimacy to a terrorist regime. Mr. Cheney further pointed out that many Democratic legislators voted against the measure. So what was the point of bringing up the question again here, without including the explanation already given? Well, of course, to plant the title of "racist" on Mr. Cheney.

    Now to the main event! As to the restroom policies: Mr. Cheney "headed" a corporation, which, along with its subsidiaries, operates in more than 100 countries. The article stated that "the company he headed for the past five years maintains separate restrooms overseas for its American and foreign employees." A Company spokesperson pointed out that their policy is

PRESS

similar to the policies in Eastern countries, which provide separate facilities for Westerners. The authors added, "And a leading public health professional said, absent evidence of unsanitary practices, he could see no justification for directing Americans and foreign hires to separate facilities." And, "A State Department official said he had never seen a similar policy in trips and assignments to four continents." Notice how the authors did not reveal who those "officials" were, nor how it was that a State Department "official" has come to be monitoring the restroom policies of foreign companies and US companies abroad? How did the reporters spend so much time finding a "public health professional" that is knowledgeable about restroom conditions in 100s of foreign countries, and not even hint as to who that person is nor mention his/her credentials?

Can we be frank here? Of course, the point of this restroom business, and the Nelson Mandela vote, was to paint Mr. Cheney as prejudiced. Does the Press identify prejudice whenever they are aware of it? Oh sure, you say, we read in the paper all the time about acts of prejudice which the Press have uncovered. Oh really!?

Pigford v. Glickman is not exactly a household term. In an informal sampling I have found nobody familiar with that case. A Federal judge approved the settlement of this case on April 15, 1999. That settlement was reported, among other places, in the New York Times and the Los Angeles Times {April 15, 1999). In the NY Times,

THE BIG LIE

it was a small article on page A29. It was a smaller article on page A11 of the LA Times.

This case has been characterized as being the only racial discrimination case ever to carry serious money damages. Determining the amount to be paid is still being calculated, but estimates are between one and two **billion** dollars. Imagine in this day and age racial discrimination being so blatant and pervasive that it warranted a billion dollars or more to settle. Fact is, settlement of the case was delayed four months so that the judge could ensure that the discrimination did not continue while the case was being settled. How can this be? How can such a huge case go by with so little notice? This is incredible!

Let's put this in perspective relative to what we have learned about the political leanings of the media elite. The Glickman in Pigford v. Glickman is Dan Glickman, President Clinton's last Secretary of Agriculture. He served as such from March, 1995 to January, 2001. Prior to that, the infamous Mike Espy served as Mr. Clinton's Secretary of Agriculture from January, 1993 to December, 1994. Truthfully, the discrimination proved in the lawsuit originated many many years before the Clinton Administration came to office. But the suit involved racially discriminatory policies up to January, 1997. And as noted, there were accusations and concerns that the practices were continuing into 1999. So, failing to correct the problem in nearly two terms of office, the axe fell on the Clinton Administration. The Press found this barely newsworthy!

PRESS

The "yah yahs" and "so whats" are answered thus: Mr. Glickman and Mr. Espy were cabinet secretaries, directly appointed by Democratic President Clinton. They were themselves Democrats. They reported directly to Mr. Clinton. He was their immediate supervisor, and would have, or surely should have been very much interested in blatant racial discrimination practiced by that Department (Agriculture). The Vice-President, Mr. Gore, should also figure prominently in here, as he surely should have had something to say about big-time racial discrimination policies of their (Clinton/Gore) Administration. But no. After the settlement, Mr. Glickman continued on in his post, apparently without a negative word from either Clinton or Gore. He should have been fired, BIG TIME, with Clinton and Gore issuing multiple apologies to all African-Americans. There should have been inquiries to determine whether or not the President was aware of those racist policies and thus needed to be held accountable. Truth is, while the Press slept on the issue, only the American taxpayers were held accountable,

The real point here is the Press. With Pigford v. Glickman fresh in mind, let's revisit the headline, "Cheney's failure to vote, **company restroom policy questioned.**" Compare, if you will, company restroom policies in foreign countries, which reportedly followed practices in those countries, with open racial discrimination in this country. Note also that the L.A. Times story about Pigford v. Glickman did not once mention

THE BIG LIE

Dan Glickman nor identify him as the Secretary of Agriculture. No mention was made of how closely he is tied to the Clinton/Gore Administration nor the fact that he reports directly to the President. The N.Y. Times article did, toward the end, include a quote from Mr. Glickman. Therein he remarked that he felt the judgment was fair. Yet, in the "restroom" incident, the Republican vice-presidential candidate is **headlined**. That, despite his being so very far removed from involvement in restroom policies of a subsidiary company in a foreign land, which policy did not involve "race" at all.

This Press propaganda is not limited to news stories. Doonesbury cartoons are certainly political cartoons. As such, they usually appear in newspaper editorial sections. It is absolutely proper that newspaper owners comment as they wish on any subject that they choose. Provided, of course, that those comments, which include political cartoons, are presented as editorials. In no way does the cartoon section denote editorial content. If the editors include editorial material in the cartoons, that is deceptive. If those "cartoon editorials" are based on bad or misleading material in order to further a certain political agenda, then they go beyond deception. They become propaganda. Misleading propaganda aimed at children. Doonesbury does appear in the Sunday cartoon section in many newspapers. Does it propagandize to push an agenda?

Perusing the Doonesbury strip during the height of the summer of 2000 presidential

PRESS

campaign illustrated the liberal bent of the author. By far, the most number of "shots" were taken at the Republican candidates, Bush and Cheney. So let's examine a couple of the most pointed strips and see if they were honest and properly in the funny papers.

The July 30, 2000 feature Doonesbury was in a radio station setting. Some early dialogue was, "Hi, folks! Mark Slackmeyer here to discuss campaign 2000's hottest topic – capital punishment." True enough, the Press was indeed pressing capital punishment as an issue. Anyway, the character continued, "Recently, Texas executed a man based solely on the testimony of a single eyewitness. Ever wonder if you have what it takes to provide critical eyewitness testimony?" The cartoon finished with the readers being asked to identify certain features of a character that appeared at the beginning of the strip.

This of course, was a jab at the Texas Governor, who was presidential candidate Bush. The reader is supposed to opine that the presidential candidate is cruel, blood thirsty, or just plain incompetent, because as Texas Governor he didn't intervene to stop that execution. Now to Gary Graham: Gary Graham? He was the fellow who was executed in Texas in June, 2000, for a murder he had committed 19 years earlier. Graham was convicted of robbing and killing Bobby Lambert. Some murders have no witnesses, some one witness, and some

THE BIG LIE

multiple witnesses. Seldom do murderers arrange an audience for their crime.

In the Graham case, Bernadine Skillern was the witness who identified him as the perpetrator. Her testimony placed him at the scene of the crime. Was it just her testimony alone that convicted Graham? Only in the funny papers! Following the aforementioned crime (the murder, not the cartoon strip), Graham went to the home of one Lisa Blackburn. Over the course of several hours he raped and robbed her. During that time, he told her that he had killed three people. Unbeknownst to Graham, Blackburn escaped from the house, with his gun, and notified the police. He was arrested in her home. He confessed to a weeklong crime spree, during which he killed two other people. Is it accurate to say that he was convicted based solely on the testimony of one eyewitness? Only if you are pushing propaganda! Remember, comedy and satire based on lies exhibit only stupidity.

After the election, the Doonesbury "cartoon" continued to swipe at President Bush. Sunday, January 28, 2001, the strip was again the scene of a radio station. Two men are talking, with the usual Doonesbury character debating a Bush person, "We're back with all things being equal!" Chase (for Bush), "Have we heard the end of Al Gore? I hope so! We've had enough of his prevarications! Who's had enough (says Slackmeyer)? The Bush oppo squad, who inflated trivial inconsistencies into lies?" Ending with, "Oh, right. Never mind that the biggest lie of the whole

PRESS

election belonged to Bush. Oh yeah? And what would that be? I won." Yes, this is the dialogue from a cartoon! It did appear in the cartoon section of newspapers.

So is there truth here? Was "I won" a lie, or is calling it a lie a lie? By the laws of the Land, Mr. Bush did win. Those who have an opinion otherwise, have just that, an opinion. Mr. Trudeau has every right to form an opinion about the matter, but his opinion does not make the prevailing contrary opinion a "lie." When he speaks thus through the forum of his cartoon strip, he is propagandizing.

The July 13, 2003, Doonesbury episode reached a pinnacle. The scene apparently is inside a newsroom. Two men are talking, and one is questioning the idea of the "liberal media." The other man states, "Drives you crazy, doesn't it? You know why? Because you liberals are hung up on fairness! You actually **try** to respect all points of view! But conservatives feel no need whatsoever to consider other views, we know we're right, so why bother? Because we have no tradition of tolerance, we're unencumbered by doubt! So we roll you guys **every** time!"

Again, the Press has every right to provide opinions, be they balanced or totally one-sided. But they belong in the editorial section. When opinions are printed as news, or cartoons, then that media is deliberately propagandizing.

By the way, did the Bush campaign "inflate trivial inconsistencies into lies?" Let's examine some.

THE BIG LIE

During the Presidential debate on October 3, 2000, Governor Bush made a comment about the good work done by FEMA during the fires and floods in Parker County, Texas. Apparently in an effort not to be upstaged by Bush, Vice President Gore stated, "I accompanied James Lee Witt (FEMA Director) down to Texas when those fires broke out." The inference being that Gore went to Texas in an official capacity regarding the devastation. The "trivial inconsistency" here was that Witt did not go to Texas to deal with the fires. Gore was in Texas for a fundraising event. Gore did not accompany Mr. Witt, nor did he visit the fire scene.[31] Hmmmm.

How about, "During my service in the United States Congress, I took the initiative in creating the internet."[32] Put that next to the Associated Press story about Vice President Gore speaking to a steel worker regarding job-training programs, "Gore smiled and admitted that he, too, has trouble turning on a computer – let alone using one."[33] So, he created the internet without even knowing how to turn on a computer? The fact that Mr. Gore had a propensity to lie when it suited a purpose was well known. Recall a New York Post headline of October 5, 2000, "Gore's nose is growing again." An interesting read is the July 5, 2000, article in the New York Times titled, "The Tale of Two Gores: A primer on the Fund-Raising Inquiry."[34] The story primarily reported on an interview of Vice President Gore by federal investigators. The topics were: Mr. Gore's appearance at a luncheon at a Buddhist temple,

PRESS

his attendance at coffees in the White House, and telephone calls from the Executive Mansion. All regarded as suspected illegal fund raising activities. The Vice President's truthfulness during the interview was questioned. For instance, Mr. Gore stated that he might have attended one White House coffee, when it was documented that he attended 23. His memory regarding the other events was vague. The outcome of the interview was that the head of the Justice Department's campaign task force recommended that the Attorney General appoint a special counsel to investigate the Vice President's veracity, particularly in light of the fact that he displayed a meticulous memory regarding other legal matters.

The liberal mainstream Press identified several self-serving lies by Mr. Gore, independent of statements from the Bush campaign. So, is it **true** that the Bush campaign inflated "trivial inconsistencies into lies," or did the Doonesbury cartoon bend and twist the truth in order to push propaganda? Obviously, the deceptive "means" was considered justified by the "end" of garnering support for the Vice President.

It is interesting to note that during the 2000 presidential campaign, Mr. Cheney lashed out at the Press. He remarked that too much of their focus is on trivial issues.[35] One might add that obviously they also neglect selected big issues.

Returning to Adolph Hitler writing in Mein Kampf: "At first I could not help but be amazed at how short a time it took this great evil power

THE BIG LIE

(Press) within the state to create a certain opinion even when it meant totally falsifying profound desires and views...In a few days a ridiculous episode had become a significant state action, while, conversely, at the same time, vital problems fell a prey to public oblivion, or rather were simply filched from the memory and consciousness of the masses."[11]

It is tragic! The role of the Press can be so instrumental in providing the knowledge necessary for people to free themselves from tyranny, and to raise their lot to new heights. But, when the Press sells itself to those who would be king and wallows in the quagmire of lies and deception, it becomes a force of evil. Then the people are forced to root out the truth as best they can. Most folks don't do that, but continue to believe in the Press, and thus ride into the camp of the Hitlers. This is facilitated by the use of slogans.

BEWARE THE ROBOTIC SLOGANEER

For many years an anomaly has plagued my mind. It involves some folks voting habits compared to their basic beliefs. I have known several people who, in the course of regular conversation, have seemed to lean toward the Right in commenting on various events. That is, they are pretty hard-line on the treatment of criminals. Some feel that the schools would be better off with stricter policies. Many really resent paying taxes when they are able to articulate witnessing waste in government spending. They also exhibit hawkish attitudes toward military policies. Having expressed these, and other seeming right wing attitudes, they consistently vote for Democrats.

Now I believe I know what is at work here. **SLOGANS**. Yes, slogans, either single word, or more often, simple expressions. One slogan, though it is basically a lie, is a powerful thing. Repeated often enough, and in the proper forum,

THE BIG LIE

can easily stomp the truth into the ground. Note also that **slogans** often are questions, asked repeatedly, to produce a perception. These frequently involve lies by omission. That is, there is a good answer to the question, but that answer is never included because then the impact is lost because the truth becomes known.

In Nazi Germany, the Reich Propaganda Office actually issued directives to "organizers" which included slogans that they were to promote. Those slogans were fitted for the demographic characteristics of the target audience. That, alone, is not evil. However, those slogans were generally not based on truth, but were lies or manipulations designed to promote their political cause. That, is evil. Hitler called it, "Work of enlightenment."[36]

To what end were these slogans? Hitler and his Nazi cohorts came to power at the peoples' request. Make no mistake, in the political circles of the early 1930's Adolph Hitler was considered a little nuisance; a blow-hard bully. He was not taken seriously. Even when he weaseled himself into a position of power, his power base was limited. That base grew with the approval of great throngs of the German people. So what tactic did he use to so firmly rise to power?

It is very difficult to be placed into a position of great power in a society of contented people. When the people do not feel as though anyone is working to keep them "down," they will give little thought to the politics of the country, or its leaders. Consider yourself rich, middle class, or even poor. You are comfortable in making a

BEWARE THE ROBOTIC SLOGANEER

living. Even if that is currently meager, you feel that you do have opportunities to advance. Your social life is not threatened, and you can move about as you please. So how much trouble are you going to go to attend a mass political rally for someone who wants to fix things for you?

For the majority of citizens, only when they feel that there is a group or faction out "to get" them, to destroy their contentment, the environment, their freedom, will they pay attention to the political scene. Of course, if a group is out to get you, and that group is more powerful then you, you will look to the government to protect you and make things right. At that point, you **will** attend the political rally for the leader who convinces you that he or she understands who is to blame for your problems and promises solutions.

The Nazis preached unity and denounced conflicts among social groups. Non-partisanship was their theme. The reality was that they worked hard to convince certain groups that there were factions out to get them. They promoted victimization. Hitler convinced the various "victimized" factions that he could solve their problems if they would just replace democracy with his leadership. Through the clever and frequent use of **slogans**, the **robotic sloganeers** did so convince enough people. And, the blood-bath began.

Are the robotic sloganeers at work in this country? Freedom. Picture a group of protesters holding hands and swaying while singing about

THE BIG LIE

"overcoming" and "freedom". Aren't these the same folks who so vociferously urge the government to increase entitlement programs, control the evil capitalists, push all politically correct environmental issues, etc. etc? History has consistently shown us that freedom diminishes in direct proportion to increases in government size and power and intrusiveness. So are these people really crying for "freedom," or is that just a slogan that sells better than "Socialism?"

Just this morning while sipping my coffee and watching the TV news, a **slogan** flowed like honey. That is, a "tax break primarily benefits the rich." Thus the poor are being victimized. This "news" comment was in response to newly elected President Bush's plan to significantly lower taxes. Of course, the Left is attacking this plan. It is difficult to recall a "news story" recently that has not in some way repeated that **slogan.** On the aforementioned news cast, a Democratic legislator was standing next to a luxury automobile, and he was holding a car muffler. He pointed out that the break given to a person with substantial income would pay for the car. A person with a much lower income would only be able to buy the muffler.

After hearing repeatedly that the tax break would primarily benefit the rich, and seeing the illustration of the car and the muffler, what is one to think? The casual observer, of which we have too many, would certainly be swayed to believe the President's proposal victimizes the poor. Even

BEWARE THE ROBOTIC SLOGANEER

if a person "leans" to the right, they could well be against anyone proposing an unfair tax cut. Surely with the illustration of the car and muffler and the oft-repeated **slogan,** the "unfairness" is true.

And what do folks believe? A CNN-Time poll was taken regarding the Bush tax cut plan. The results were reported in the media February 10, 2001. The poll asked, "Do you think Bush's tax cut proposals, if passed, would favor the rich more than the poor, the poor more than the rich, or would they be fair to all Americans?" 51% said it would favor the rich, 6% went for favor the poor, and 35% thought it would be fair.[37]

Significance? The basic plan calls for a 33% reduction in the lowest tax bracket, and a 16.5% cut in the highest (15% to 10%, and 39.6% to 33%). There are other reductions relating to the marriage penalty, childcare credit, educational savings accounts, etc. These would suggest more benefits to younger, lower income groups.

OK, so the unfairness "slogan" refers to the final dollar amount of the savings, not the percentage. That is, with that 16.5% reduction a person paying $20,000 per year tax would save $3,300. With the 33% cut, a person paying $1,000 per year would only save $330. There's just one thing missing here. Those who are calling for fairness in the dollar amount are forgetting to call for fairness both ways. That is, fairness in the amount each group is paying, as well as receiving reductions. Fairness here would be that each of the above taxpayers would have been paying

THE BIG LIE

$10,500 per year, with each receiving the same amount of reduction.

A letter to the editor in today's paper accuses President Bush of being a liar when the President projects his tax cut proposal will benefit families the most. Primarily he bemoans his perception that the higher tax bracket will receive a larger "percentage" reduction (16.5%) then will the lower (33%)?[38] The writer ignored several tax cut provisions aimed at childcare, education, and families. Here we have a prime example of robotic **sloganeering**. Never mind the facts, the "work of enlightenment" has been accomplished!

One final word here about tax cuts and slogans attached thereto. Tax cuts are often characterized as money taken from the Treasury and given, mostly, to the rich. Tax cuts are not Treasury funds paid in by us working folk and plundered to pay the rich. Tax cuts result in taxpayers simply having to pay a smaller percentage of their income to the Government in the future. This juvenile explanation is in response to the February 19, 2001 Newsweek magazine cover. The headline read: "Tax Cuts & You. Bush's $1.6 Trillion Gamble." Prominently pictured was President Bush with two hands-full of new $100 bills. He is broadly smiling and handing the money toward the reader. Of course, the impression conveyed is that the President is taking huge sums of money out of the Treasury and handing them out. That is deceptive **sloganeering** designed to "enlighten," subtle as it may be.

BEWARE THE ROBOTIC SLOGANEER

Too often slogans are used to unjustly tag a person with the label of racist. In a prior chapter the Dick Cheney/Nelson Mandela matter was raised. It is a prime example of how a "question" can be used as a **slogan** to label a person. In 1986 then Representative Dick Cheney voted against a resolution before the House that among other things called for the release of South African leader Nelson Mandela. "Among other things" is key here. The fact is the resolution also called for the US Government to recognize the African National Congress. The ANC was then a terrorist organization largely controlled by Marxists. They had close ties with the likes of Fidel Castro and Muammar Khadafy. Remember the "necklacing" activities they applied to their political opponents? They would fill a tire with gasoline, place it over the head of a victim, and then light it. They reportedly ran torture centers in other countries in Africa. Mr. Cheney has explained that of course he wanted Mandela freed. But the resolution would not have any legal force in South Africa, causing him to be freed, but it could have given comfort and aid to a then terrorist organization. Note that 32 Democrats voted along with a host of Republicans to defeat the measure.

During the 2000 presidential campaign, a seemingly outraged President and Mrs. Clinton joined the **sloganeering** and were quoted as saying, "an amazing vote…that takes your breath away…It's hard to explain no matter how hard (Cheney) tries."[39]

THE BIG LIE

Bill Nelson is a Democrat from Florida who at the same time was running for a Senate seat. In 1986, Mr. Nelson, as a member of Congress, was among the 32 Democrats who voted against the resolution. His spokesman explained, "Bottom line is that Nelson strongly supported two components of the measure, and he considers Mandela one of the century's great leaders. He could not support the third, recognizing ANC because it was dominated by the communist party. This vote should be looked at in context."[40] Shortly after making the "breath away" remark, Mr. Clinton talked about Mr. Nelson. He said, "I want to say that I'm honored to be here for Bill Nelson…And we've had the opportunity over the years at various encounters to get to know one another…I think we need more people like them in Washington, people who are civil and decent and reasonable and caring, and not just in election season, not just as a part of a marketing strategy, but because they think it's the right thing to do."[41] Time and again, "news stories" and campaigning Democrats repeated the **slogan** regarding Mr. Cheney's Mandela vote. Obviously that was done to paint him as a racist. Throw out a slogan often enough, and people will believe it. To fully grasp the import here, the reader is invited to tap the Internet. Search Cheney/Mandela, and see how many times during the 2000 presidential campaign this subject is brought up in magazines and the Press. Only a few publications that alluded to Mr. Cheney's vote carried the explanation for it. Likewise, the fact that many

BEWARE THE ROBOTIC SLOGANEER

Democrats voted the same way is not mentioned. Is that lying by omission?

To put this in proper perspective, let's compare the Cheney vote to the Pigford v. Glickman case. Stunning, huh? So, is the left wing, including the mainstream Press, really concerned and outraged about racial prejudice? Or, do they just use it, true or not, to propagandize? The **robotic sloganeers** are at work, and they do not need the truth in order to operate.

These are just a couple of in-depth looks at slogans flooding our information ways that are or were intended to paint certain societal groups as victims. There is no shortage of slogans that are intended not to educate, but to indoctrinate. Here are some more:

How about the pharmaceutical industry is ripping off the consumers by making huge profits? No less than President Clinton said, "The pharmaceutical industry is spending $1 billion more each year on advertising and lobbying than it does on developing new and better drugs. Meanwhile, its profits are rising at four times the rate of the average Fortune 500 company."[42] The drug industry spends about an equal amount on promotions as it does on development. Most industries spend a much larger percentage on their promotions. The drug industry has to spend an inordinate amount just to get approval of their products. A very small percentage of products tested actually make it to market. Fact is, pharmaceutical industry profits are in line with

THE BIG LIE

other industries. But, attacking them creates a whole batch of "victims." Victims with a problem that can be cured, "If you will simply vote for me."

Remember reading about the "shocking" display of racial discrimination among mortgage lenders? Mortgage companies are rejecting blacks for home mortgages at a higher rate than they are whites. What is the truth? Actually, Asians are declined less often then are whites. So are there truly different standards being applied to loan applications? That could be difficult to prove. However, we can get a pretty clear view by coming in the back door. That is, look at the rate of mortgage defaults. If the accusation were true, default rates would be the highest among Asians, and lowest among blacks. 'Taint so! The rates are even enough to lead us to believe that the mortgage companies are doing a good and prudent job screening loan applications, and being color-blind while doing so. They DO need to protect our savings accounts.

Even technical journals get into the sloganeering act. From the January, 2001 Scientific American magazine: An article by Rodger Doyle concerned illegal drug use in this country. He pointed out that the Anti-Drug Abuse Act of 1986 specified that the penalty for possession of 5 grams of crack would be the same as that for possessing 500 grams of powder cocaine. So far so good, but now the **sloganeering**. "African-Americans were much more likely than whites to use crack, and so…came under greater obloquy". This being a

BEWARE THE ROBOTIC SLOGANEER

"scientific" magazine the use of obscure words is acceptable. Unfortunately so is the use of phantom facts. Though the article is replete with graphs and statistical data, that "African-Americans were more likely than whites to use crack" was an unsupported opinion cleverly slipped in. Going on in the article, "Because of the powder cocaine/crack penalty differential and other inequities in the justice system, blacks were far more likely to go to prison for drug offenses than whites, even though use of illicit drugs overall was about the same among both races. Blacks account for 13 percent of those who use illegal drugs but 74 percent of those sentenced to prison for possession."

OK, what are the "inequities of the justice system?" Another unsubstantiated **slogan** aimed at victimizing, perhaps? Oh sure, we have heard the endless **slogans** lamenting how poor and/or black people are unfairly treated by the legal system. Some time ago African-American Professor/author Walter Williams addressed this issue. He invited us to go to black communities in the Bronx, Harlem, or North Philadelphia. Ask folks there, in these crime-ridden neighborhoods, which they fear. The answer won't be "the police" or "white people". Prof. Williams went on, "Blame for the current state of affairs, in reality, lies in the tolerance of the court toward criminals and in the support that black leadership gives to the criminal element of the black community."[43]

Back to the Scientific American article: The "use of illicit drugs overall was about the same

THE BIG LIE

among both races." This story isn't complete without throwing that in. Was there data to support this "fact?" Not in this "scientific" journal. "Blacks account for 13 percent of those who use illegal drugs but 74 percent of those sentenced to prison." Here again, we have numbers that should outrage any reasonable person. So, where did the numbers 13% and 74% come from? That was not footnoted in the article. Asked to accept that they are true, what point is proven? Doesn't the number sentenced desperately need some other facts to be worth even mentioning? We need to know how many people were arrested for a number sentenced to have meaning. Other factors would be the economic factors that may account for users being more or less exposed to law enforcement. Sentencing would depend not just on being found guilty, but also on past criminal records.

The upshot is, this "scientific" article took great liberties by injecting pointless numbers and unsubstantiated figures and "opinions." No doubt, the author felt that the end of once again painting African-Americans as victims justified the means. Ah yes, left wing **sloganeering**.

The Reagan presidency provided an excellent venue for observing robotic sloganeering. Volumes have been written correcting the myths that emanated from the mainstream press and other news carriers. Remember hearing that government spending on social programs decreased by huge percentages? Fact is, in dollars, as well as in percentage of Gross

BEWARE THE ROBOTIC SLOGANEER

National Product, social spending increased during that Administration.

Of course, via news stories and editorials in the most visible media, we know that the Reagan years (1980s) were especially tough on African-Americans and other minorities. Fact is between 1978 and 1982 the poverty rate for Blacks rose 14% and for Hispanics 27.8%. Between 1982 and 1989, the rate decreased for Blacks, 13.7% and for Hispanics, 12.3%.[44]

Here is a good objective story: "Middle-class families can't buy a house because they're too busy paying for people to have mansions in Chevy Chase, second houses in Malibu, and empty office buildings everywhere." C. Austin Fitts, former federal housing commissioner, quoted in The National Journal, June 22, 1991. Fact is, housing affordability during the Carter Administration absolutely tanked. Soaring inflation and mortgage rates made homes less and less affordable. During the Reagan years, the Housing Affordability Index rose from a dismal 68.9 in 1981 to 122 in 1988. An index of 100 means that a family with a median income can purchase a median-priced home. The economics of home buying improves as the index goes upward. Reagan policies causing dramatically reduced inflation and reduced interest rates accounted for much of this success.

Let's return to tax cuts. What a great subject for **sloganeering**. "They favor the rich at the expense of the poor. They will cause the Social Security system to crash. They will be responsible

THE BIG LIE

for the deaths of numerous children." We've heard them all, right? Well not quite. Here is a classic example which shows how **sloganeering** can be used, no matter how far fetched.

In the early summer of 2003, the Maine Department of Transportation discovered some major safety problems with a 72-year-old span bridge. The bridge is on Coast Route 1, and carries a lot of tourist traffic traveling to visit Bar Harbor and Acadia National Park. It crosses the mighty Penobscot River, south of Bangor. A Bangor Daily News article on July 14, 2003 carried a follow-up story reporting that truck travel had been banned on the bridge. Numerous safety concerns were cited as the reason, and there were even hints that the bridge may have to be closed to all traffic.

Of course, a number of local business and government leaders were speaking out about the problems to be anticipated. One Waldo County commissioner was particularly critical. He said the State should not have waited 72 years to conduct a major inspection. That seemed like a reasonable criticism. But then the commissioner became a **robotic sloganeer** by fixing the blame on "tax cut after tax cut after tax cut, and you send billions of dollars to Iraq." With the Presidential campaigns beginning to heat up, the Democrats are apparently going to attack President Bush on the economy by predicting economic woes from his tax cuts. Of course, the left has consistently been against the war in Iraq.

BEWARE THE ROBOTIC SLOGANEER

So, tax cut and anti-war slogans are to be expected. But whoa!

It has been a well-publicized fact that Maine residents are the highest taxed in the Union. From that perspective, there being "tax cut after tax cut" is a hard concept to swallow. The war in Iraq has been going on now for about four months. So, what percentage of 72 years does that represent? No, the Commissioner just threw in those slogans off the cuff. He probably would have done so, no matter what the subject.

But here's the real insidious part. The newspaper article was replete with pictures, as well as interviews with a number of folks. But the editor chose to caption the commissioner's tax cut and war-cost statements. Did the editor find the President's **proposed** tax cut a real factor in the deterioration of this bridge and the fact it hadn't been inspected in the past? Have the war costs of the past few months really prevented proper inspections for 72 years? No, like the commissioner, the paper staff saw an opportunity to throw out a bit of propaganda to support their agenda.

Pesticide spraying provides fertile ground for sloganeering. An editorial piece in the July 10, 2003, Ellsworth American newspaper epitomized this subject. The writer wrote of the doom and gloom we are and will be facing due to agricultural pesticide spraying. She cited cancer clusters that she surmised were a direct result of blueberry field spraying. The fact that research has failed to find that connection was decried as ridiculous.

THE BIG LIE

She said that the greedy chemical companies are doping farmers into applying chemicals. We've all heard this tune many times, right? Let's look at some facts:

Though that writer was referencing pesticide use in Maine, similar cries have been heard in the rich farm belt in Central California. Both areas have reported "cancer clusters," which have been investigated by medical teams. Reports from these investigations have questioned the "cluster" aspect, and they have found no real connection to pesticide use. A big conspiracy, no doubt.

Seriously, consider this, referencing the Central California farm belt: A good percentage of farmers live on their farms. Many of those do some, if not all of their own pesticide spraying. These materials swirl around them, drift into their yards, onto their gardens, and presumably washed into their drinking water. So, with this extreme exposure, certainly there must be a high rate of cancer among these farmers. Well, no, no "cancer cluster" exists here. How can that be?

Are farmers being duped by "greedy chemical companies" to use their pesticides unnecessarily? I do not know of a single farmer (and I know quite a few) who likes to spend money needlessly. Pesticide applications are expensive and take a big bite out of farm income. In fact, farmers are always looking for ways of reducing their spraying expenses.

Agricultural spraying has come to be during the past century. Know what else has occurred during that time? The life expectancy of people in

BEWARE THE ROBOTIC SLOGANEER

this country has taken a dramatic leap up. Could this be due to the increased availability of produce for our diets, at reasonable prices, due to better insect and weed control?

It is true that there are some diseases, such as some cancers and other ailments, which are on the increase in this country. Lots of good scientific data seems to indicate that there is a common cause for these increases. A cause which indeed is reaching epidemic proportions. It has been very much in the news lately. That cause is obesity! Perhaps we would be better served if our tables contained a lot less hysteria, and more servings of farm-grown fruits and vegetables. But that would fail to address the need for the left wing to sloganeer against the capitalist agricultural interests.

The point is, of course, that **sloganeering** is a tool for political propaganda when it is based on lies or twisted facts. It serves no good purpose when it rises from the ashes of burned truths. Those who propagate these slogans do so for an evil purpose. That just follows, as there is no need for such deception in noble purposes.

Anyone finding himself or herself being a **robotic sloganeer** must look into a mirror and initiate some evaluation. Do you refer to left wing radicals as right wingers? Do you utter other **slogans** that clearly are meant to focus a false impression on a political ideology? If so, your political agenda needs some real scrutiny. If your position(s) has to be supported by a lie, your position needs to be reexamined. The

THE BIG LIE

significance is not in the scope of the lie, but in the need to lie.

LIST OF REFERENCES

1. Spielvogel, Jackson J. *Hitler and Nazi Germany: A History.* Englewood Cliffs, New Jersey: Prentice Hall. 1988.

2. Hitler, Adolph. *Mein Kampf.* First Mariner Books, Edition 1999. The Houghton Mifflin Company.

3. Spielvogel, Jackson J. *Hitler and Nazi Germany: A History.*

4. Hertzstein, Robert Edwin. *The Nazis World War II.* Alexandria, Virginia. Time-Life Books – Time Inc. 1980.

5. Ibid.

6. Ibid.

7. Ibid.

8. Falcoff, Mark. *Peron's Nazi Ties.* Time International Vol 152, Nov. 9, 1998.

9. Alexander, Robert J. *The Peron Era.* New York. Columbia University Press. 1951

10. *Latin American Dictatorships – And After The Challenge Of The Past.* The Economist. Oct. 24, 1998.

11. *Can't Erase This.* Newsweek. Vol 125 Mar. 17, 1995.

12. Alexander, Robert J. *The Peron Era.*

13. Diederich, Bernard. *Somoza.* New York. Elsevier-Dutton Publishing Co., 1981.

14. Rudolph, James D. ed. US Government, Secretary of the Army. *Nicaragua A Country Study.* 1982.

15. Diederich, Bernard. *Somoza.*

16. Van Toai, Doan, and David Chanoff. *The Vietnamese Gulag.* New York, Simon & Schuster, 1986.

17. Kolko, Gabriel. *Anatomy of a War. Vietnam.* New York. Pantheon Books, 1985

18. Ibid.

LIST OF REFERENCES

19. Speilvogel, Jackson. *Western Civilization.* Vol.II. St. Paul, MN. West Publishing Co. 1994.

20. Ibid.

21. Hitler, Adolph. *Mein Kampf.*

22. Ibid.

23. Ibid.

24. Barnes, Fred. *Can We Trust The News.* Reader's Digest. Jan. 1988

25. Lichter, S. Robert, Stanley Rothman, and Linda S. Lichter. *The Media Elite.* Bethesda, MD. Adler & Adler, 1986.

26. Barnes, Fred. *Can We Trust The News.*

27. Lichter, S. Robert, Stanley Rothman, and Linda S. Lichter. *The Media Elite.*

28. The Chicago Tribune, June 17, 1998.

29. The News With Brian Williams. Fox News. Sep. 18, 2000.

30. The New York Times. Aug. 12, 2000.

31. New York Post. Oct. 5, 2000.

32. Transcript. www.wired.com/news/news/politics/story/18390 HTML.

33. Associated Press. Sep. 4, 1998

34. Van Natta Jr., Don and David Johnston. The New York Times. Jul 5, 2000.

35. The Fresno Bee, Sep. 14, 2000.

36. Hitler, Adolph. *Mein Kampf.*

37. Fram, Alan. Associated Press. Feb. 10, 2001.

38. The Fresno Bee. Feb. 12, 2001.

39. New York Post. Aug. 7, 2000.

40. Hayes, Stephen F. National Review. Jul. 31, 2000.

41. Ibid.

42. National Review. Mar. 29, 1993.

43. Williams, Walter E. *Black Leaders Tell Only Part of the Story.* Human Events. Jan. 10, 1981.

44. Census Bureau. *Poverty in the US.* U.S. Government. Aug., 1991.

ABOUT THE AUTHOR

Dale Sprinkle's life gives new meaning to the term "well rounded". He has had careers in law enforcement (LAPD), grape farming, and real estate appraising. Dale is a commercially licensed pilot, certified SCUBA diver, expert skier, and competition runner.

He has had extensive research and technical writing experience starting with his assignment as the secretary to a commanding general while serving in the Marine Corps. Dale was assigned to a variety of positions within the LAPD, including Planning and Research. Dale quips that he received a great deal of fiction writing experience during this assignment composing budget and position justifications. Dale credits law school, which he graduated from in 1972, with helping him hone his research skills.

Printed in the United Kingdom
by Lightning Source UK Ltd.
122176UK00001B/101/A